Eyewitness Accounts of the American Revolution

Occupation of New York City by the British

Ewald Gustav Schaukirk

The New York Times & Arno Press

[*Reprinted from the Pennsylvania Magazine of History and Biography
for January, 1887.*]

OCCUPATION OF NEW YORK CITY BY THE BRITISH.

[Under the above caption, in Nos. 2 and 3 of Vol. I., PENNA. MAG. HIST. AND BIOG., we reprinted extracts from the diary of the Moravian congregation in the city of New York, for the year 1776, which had been prepared for *The Moravian*, by Rt. Rev. A. A. Reinke. The excerpts now presented begin with the year 1775 and end with 1783,— excepting 1778, the MS. of which is missing.

Ewald Gustav Schaukirk, the diarist, was born 28th February, 1725, at Stettin, Prussia, where his father was a lawyer and member of the town council. Uniting with the Moravian Church, and entering its ministry, he filled positions on the Continent and Great Britain, and in the mission among the negroes in the West Indies. In the summer of 1774 he was sent to America, and the year following was appointed pastor of the New York congregation, where he remained until 1784. The church, a brick building, stood on Fair, now Fulton, between Nassau and William Streets, and was dedicated June 18, 1752. The parsonage adjoined. Mr. Schaukirk was consecrated a bishop in 1785, and died at Herrnhut, Saxony, March 19, 1805.—ED.]

1775.

February 28th. Tuesday.—About noon, the new Hospital, not quite finished, was consumed by fire.[1]

March 6th. Monday.—A noisy day, owing to the election of Delegates to the Provincial Congress.

April 23d. Sunday.—The reports from Boston that hostilities had begun between the King's troops and the Provincials,[2] created considerable commotion.

April 29th. Saturday.—The past week has been one of commotion and confusion. Trade and public business was at a stand; soldiers were enlisted; the inhabitants seized

---

[1] The hospital at Reneleagh caught fire while the workmen were at dinner, and the wooden portion of the building was destroyed in about one hour.

[2] Skirmish at Lexington, April 19.

the keys of the Custom House; and the arms and powder were taken from the Corporation. Fear and panic seized many of the people, who prepared to move into the country.

May 26th. Friday.—This evening we were notified that the Provincial Congress[1] had directed that all clergymen who preach in English, are in turn to open the sessions with prayers.

June 6th. Tuesday.—The King's troops were embarked on a man-of-war for Boston.

June 25th. Sunday.—Considerable excitement in Town. Our Governor, William Tryon, was expected today from England; and also General Washington of the Provincials, who has been appointed Commander-in-chief of all the troops by the Continental Congress. Some regard would be shown to the Governor, but the chief attention was paid to Gen. Washington.[2] The Governor landed late in the evening.

June 26th. Monday.—Gen. Washington left for New England, amid great pomp and show.[3]

August 24th. Thursday.—Last evening was one of excitement. About midnight some of the town-soldiers began to remove the cannon from the Battery. The Asia,[4] man-of-war watched their movements. Capt Vandeput, who is a humane man, and had no intention to injure the city, but was determined to protect the King's property, fired a couple of guns. His barge and the citizens fired on each other—one of the barge men was killed, and on both sides some were wounded. The firing alarmed the citizens, drums were beat and the soldiers assembled. Twenty one

[1] Convened at the Exchange, foot of Broad Street, on 22d inst.

[2] Washington, attended by Generals Schuyler and Lee, and escorted by the "First City Troop," in command of Captain Markoe, reached the city in the afternoon, where he was received by the military and citizens.

[3] The "City Troop" escorted Washington as far as King's Bridge, and returned to New York on Tuesday evening. They set out for Philadelphia on Thursday.

[4] The "Asia," 64, George Vandeput, commander, arrived from Boston, **May 26.**

cannons were secured. The Asia then fired a broadside with ball, which damaged several houses.[1]

August 25th. Friday.—The excitement unabated and removals from the city continue to be made. A correspondence has been carried on between the Captain of the Asia and the Mayor, and through the latter with the Committee of the " One Hundred," to adjust matters. Gov. Tryon acted as mediator.[2]

August 28th. Monday.—Moving out of the city continues, and some of the Streets look plague-stricken, so many houses are closed. The dividing of all men between 16 and 50 years into Ward companies, increases the movement.

September 18th. Monday.—The Minute men paraded today, with their baggage and provisions. It was thought they were going on an expedition, but they marched but five miles out of the city and returned in the evening. Many of them got drunk, fought together where they had halted, and on their return the Doctors and Surgeons were kept busy. May the Lord have mercy on this poor City !

October 10th. Tuesday.—On account of an attempt which has been made to take blankets, sheets, &c., from the King's Store, the City is again in danger of being fired upon. The goods taken were subsequently carried back. It is observed that some of the " Head-men" of the City begin to hang their heads down, and many believe they will be ruined men !

October 16th. Monday.—The report that all the Crown officers and our Governor are to be arrested, caused Gov. Tryon to write a letter to the Mayor, which appeared in print. This caused fresh alarm.[3]

October 19th. Thursday.—This afternoon a Captain of the rifle company which recently marched through Bethlehem, and was returning from Cambridge, died here, and was interred in Trinity Church yard with military honors.[4] Gov.

---

[1] *New York Gazette*, August 28.   [2] Ibid.   [3] Ibid., October 23.

[4] Captain Michael Cresap, of the First Regiment Riflemen. His company marched through Bethlehem, July 28. For order of funeral procession, see *N. Y. Gazette*, October 23.

Tryon went on board the Sloop-of-war Halifax, not deeming it safe to remain in the city.

November 3rd. Thursday.—In the city there were again disturbances.[1]

1777.

January 7th. Tuesday.—Since the attack and defeat which the Hessians sustained near Trenton, the rebels are again in high spirits; and whereas the King's troops have been ordered down towards Philadelphia from Newark and Hackensack, the rebels are come again to these places, and distress the people greatly.

January 14th. Tuesday.—At the request of Gen. Howe, we loaned several wagon loads of our benches for the entertainment to be held on the Queen's birthday.[2]

January 18th. Saturday.—Reports prevailed that a part of the rebel army was approaching the city, and early this morning they had made an attack upon a fort above King's Bridge, but were repulsed.

January 20th. Monday.—It appears from the newspapers, that another attempt to destroy the city by fire would be made. The city watch was regulated anew, by which eighty men watched every night in the different wards; and the Light Horse patrol the streets. Today a beginning was made with the inhabitants to take the oath of allegiance to the King. Every day two wards are taken—the Governor, Mayor, and other officers being present.

March 4th. Thursday.—This afternoon Dr. Auchmuty, Rector of Trinity Church, who died on Tuesday, was buried in St. Pauls. Mr. Inglis kept the services. The attendance

---

[1] Attack of Captain Sears on Rivington's *Royal Gazetteer* printing-office, at the foot of Wall Street.

[2] January 18, being the Queen's birthday, a royal salute was fired at Fort St. George; his Majesty's Commissioners gave a grand entertainment to the Governor, officers of the army and navy, both British and Hessian, and in the evening an exhibition of fireworks, under direction of Captain Montresor. Sir William Howe gave an elegant ball and supper; the former was opened by Mrs. Clark and Governor Tryon.

was large, notwithstanding the weather [rainy and snowy] was very bad.[1]

March 18th. Tuesday.—On Sunday night about 100 rebels being in a house near King's Bridge, some of the King's troops went to capture them. As they entered the house they were fired upon, and the captain and four or five of his men were killed. Forty of the rebels were killed and the others taken prisoners.[2]

May 29th. Wednesday.—The King's troops are preparing for the campaign. The day before yesterday some of the fleet with fresh troops arrived, and yesterday a large number of troops came in from King's Bridge to embark.

May 31st. Saturday.—As many troops have arrived, some were lodged in the North Church[3] opposite us, (who were very noisy), others in the Methodist[4] meeting-house and in the Old Dutch Church.[5]

June 5th. Thursday.—Troops are constantly being moved.

June 6th. Friday.—Large bodies of troops have been sent into the Jerseys—more German troops arrived.[6] The Hospital Ship having received sailing orders, Dr. Edmonton (who lodges with us) the other doctors and surgeons, and Dr. Morris, the chief, who lodged in our neighborhood, hurried on board with their baggage.

June 25th. Wednesday.—A rumor states, that the expedition of the army had not succeeded—the enemy were too strongly entrenched—and they returned to Amboy. Since their return our streets have been filling up.

June 28th. Saturday.—Since Thursday a report has prevailed that there had been a smart battle in the Jerseys. After the King's troops had embarked and the day appointed for the sailing of the expedition, the general received intel-

[1] *N. Y. Gazette*, March 10.   [2] Ibid., March 24.

[3] Whenever the diarist uses the term "North Church," he refers to the North Dutch Church, corner Fulton and William Streets, at one time occupied by the Post-Office.

[4] John, near Nassau Street, known as the "Old John Street Church."

[5] Garden Street, or "South Dutch Church."

[6] The First Division of the Margrave of Anspach and Baireuth, and Chasseurs, and a body of Hessian Yagers.

ligence that the rebel army was within three miles of Amboy. The troops were disembarked, and marched in the night to surprise Washington. The reports vary much : 1000 killed of the King's troops ; 5 or 6000 of the rebels, as many taken prisoners, with their artillery ; Washington was among the slain, Stirling dead of his wounds, Gov. Livingston likewise ; 400 Pennsylvanians had grounded their arms and come over to the regulars. Seventy were taken prisoners, who together with a couple of field-pieces, were brought to the city.[1] Matters go but slow, and cause concern to all disinterested well-wishers.

July 1st. Tuesday.—The North Church appears to be used again, either as a Hospital or a Prison.

July 3d. Thursday.—The King's troops have returned to Staten Island from Jersey. The rebels have now the whole Jerseys again, except Powles Hook, [now Jersey City] and we are just where we were last year, after being in possession of New York Island. It is very discouraging !

July 14th. Monday.—Gen. Prescott who had the command in NewPort, has been taken by the rebels ; being it is said in his country house. A great oversight ![2]

July 22d. Tuesday.—Yesterday a report prevailed that Gen. Burgoyne has taken Ticonderoga, and is advancing with his army.

July 23d. Wednesday.—It is reported that the Fleet has sailed from the Hook ; and that Washington is near King's Bridge.

August 22d. Friday.—There is considerable alarm on account of the rebels having been on Staten Island, destroyed the forage, plundered many of the inhabitants and had a smart fight, in which many were killed and taken prisoners on both sides. It is surprising that they should not be better on their guard. The King's troops have doubtless lost more than they will own.[3]

August 31st. Sunday.—In the city it has been sickly this month ; many people, especially children died. On many evenings 7 or 8 were buried, and on one in particular seven-

[1] *N. Y. Gazette*, June 30.　　[2] Ibid., July 21.　　[3] Ibid., September 1.

teen. As to the war, little has been done as yet; people begin to speak loudly that the commanders don't do what they might, and seem to protract rather than make an end of these calamities. There is a report that Burgoyne has met with a loss above Albany! Provisions here grow dearer, and the outlook for next Winter is gloomy. If there is no opening up the North River wood &c., will be an exceedingly scarce article to obtain.

September 25th. Friday.—Yesterday, but chiefly today, a fleet came in from England with some thousands of troops, and Gen. Robertson with other officers.[1] Late this evening a captain of the man-of-war Zebra, the Honl. J. Tollemache, and Capt. Pennington of the Guards, fought a duel with swords in a upper room at Hull's Tavern. The former drop'd dead, the latter received several wounds.[2]

October 3rd. Friday.—Troops and Commodore Hotham with transports, went up the North River.

October 6th. Monday.—This afternoon we heard that Fort Montgomery and the other fort had been taken by storm. Many of the King's troops were killed and wounded; among the former four Field Officers. Of the rebels, who were reckoned to be 1200, those that were not killed or made their escape, were taken prisoners.[3]

October 11th. Saturday.—Today the rebel prisoners were brought in. Near 200 of the privates passed our door and were confined in the North Church.

---

[1] Among those who arrived were Major-Generals Robertson, Wilson, Patterson, Lord Cathcart, Marquis of Lindsay, and James Rivington.

> " Rivington is arrived—let every man
> This injur'd Person's worth Confess;
> His loyal Heart abhor'd the Rebel's Plan,
> And boldly dar'd them with his Press."

[2] Hon. J. Tollemache, a brother of Earl Dysart, and Captain Pennington, son of Sir Ralph Pennington. The former was pierced through the heart and died immediately; the latter received seven wounds. Captain Tollemache's remains were buried in Trinity Churchyard on Saturday evening following.

[3] *N. Y. Gazette*, October 13.

October 24*th. Friday.*—All the prisoners taken from the North Church, and put on a man-of-war.

October 25*th. Saturday.*—Today, as well as yesterday, thousands of troops (some from Rhode Island and others from the forts) were embarked for Philadelphia. At the end of the month very bad accounts reached here from the Northern Army; Burgoyne and his troops are made prisoners; therefore Sir Henry Clinton and army went no higher up than Red Hook. They burnt Esopus and many houses, and returned hither, and are going to Philadelphia.[1]

November 29*th. Saturday.*—This week there have been several alarming circumstances:

A plot was discovered that many here (it is said there has been prepared a list of 300 to be arrested) had been enlisted for the rebel service, and intended to fall on the city within or set it on fire, when an attack was made on the island by the rebels. Several were arrested, one Mott and wife, in the Bowery; a shoemaker; a saddler; a milkman; and Skimmey, a tailor, who made his escape.

The rebels landed at Bloomingdale on this island, five miles from the city, and burnt Gen. De Lancey's house, and it is said made one officer prisoner.[2]

The rebels landed on Staten Island again, which caused great alarm. How to account for all these matters, and the poor out-look to defend what we have is difficult.

From Philadelphia came the news that Mud Island and Red Bank had been taken, but also that the Augusta 64, and another frigate had been destroyed in the Delaware, some say by accident. Things look dark every where.

December 27*th. Saturday.*—Some of the troops returned from Philadelphia. We heard that provisions were very scarce and high there: a quarter of mutton, one guinea; butter 6–8 shillings; and Ship's Bread sells freely in place of the ordinary kind.

---

[1] *N. Y. Gazette*, November 3.   [2] Ibid.

1779.

January 12*th. Tuesday.*—The arrival of the fleet from Cork was a great mercy, as provisions for the army grew very scarce and allowances had been shortened. Twelve sails also arrived from Halifax with stores and provisions. It is to be hoped that this will render some articles, particularly flour, cheaper for the inhabitants, for the exorbitant prices charged caused distress.

February 27*th. Saturday.*—On Wednesday evening some troops went over to Elizabethtown and returned the next day. The object to capture the rebel Gen. Maxwell and his brigade miscarried. Some stores were destroyed and a few prisoners brought in.

May 22*d. Saturday.*—Accounts have been received of the success of the expedition to Virginia; the loss of Pondicherry by the French, gives hopes that the French must drop their alliance with America, and that the Americans must submit. From all sides there is a better aspect now than ever before. Troops have also been in the Jerseys. Little opposition is made on the other side at present, it appears their resources fail them greatly.

July 16*th. Friday.*—News reached the city that the rebels had surprised the fort at Stony Point, up the North River, and taken it; with the addition that they had put the whole garrison to the sword, which made the account more alarming.[1]

July 21*st. Wednesday.*—Lord Cornwallis and his company arrived from England in the Greyhound.[2]

July 23*d. Friday.*—The fort at Stony Point has been evacuated by the rebels and our troops took possession on Monday last. However it has been a bad stroke, a loss of several hundred men to our army.[3]

August 19*th. Thursday.*—Early this morning the rebels

---

[1] *N. Y. Gazette*, July 19.

[2] Lord Cornwallis, Brigadier-General Paterson, and Lieutenant-Colonel Charles Stuart, of the Cameronian Regiment. Captain Dickson commanded the "Greyhound."

[3] *N. Y. Gazette*, July 26.

*

made an attack on Powles Hook. The reports vary, but they have again taken some of our people prisoners. Another instance of the great carelessness on our side, when on the other hand the military gentlemen amuse themselves with trifles and diversions.[1] Recently the walk by the ruins of Trinity Church and its grave-yard has been railed in and painted green; benches placed there and many lamps fixed in the trees, for gentlemen and ladies to walk and sit there in the evening. A band plays while the commander is present, and a sentry is placed there, that none of the common people may intrude. A paltry affair! A house opposite is adapted to accommodate the ladies or officer's women, while many honest people, both of the inhabitants and Refugees cannot get a house or lodging to live in or get their living. Such things make us sigh to the Lord that He would have mercy on this land, and make an end of these calamities and the many iniquitous practices. Murders have been perpetrated again lately.

August 25*th. Wednesday.*—Admiral Arbuthnot with his fleet and transports came up into the rivers, which caused great satisfaction. The Russel 74, with money for the army, arrived on the 23rd.

September 11*th. Saturday.*—This week two English and two Hessian regiments sailed from hence. According to report, a violent gale scattered their vessels, some were lost and others captured by the rebels. But a few reached this port again.

September 22*d. Wednesday.*—This being Coronation Day, at noon there was great firing at the Battery, which recently has been repaired and supplied with guns. At night there was a display of fire-works from the shipping.[2]

September 30*th.*—The report towards the end of the month

---

[1] *N. Y. Gazette,* August 23.

[2] The pyrotechnic display embraced the following: "King and Queen illuminated; Royal Salute of Maroons; 12 Sky Rockets; 2 Yew Trees, brilliant fire; 2 illuminated Air Balloons; 2 Tourballoons; 2 illuminated Vertical Wheels; Flight of small Rockets; Spiral Wheels; Chinese Fountain; 2 Cascades of brilliant fire, with two nests of serpents and a Swarm box &c."

of a French fleet coming, was the cause for repairing and enlarging the batteries and forts near the city, especially that on Governor's Island. Two large new forts were also made, one on Long Island opposite the city, and the other a short distance from the city, near the North River. Great sickness prevails.[1]

October 18*th. Monday.*—Of late we are under some apprehension that our chapel might be taken for a hospital. The old Dutch Church, the only one in use for the Dutch, has been desired, and at the end of this week will be taken for that purpose.

October 30*th. Saturday.*—This week all the troops returned from Rhode Island, which they evacuated. This affair caused various reflections and sensations. Stony Point has been evacuated too, so that now the city is filled with troops from every direction.

November 19*th. Friday.*—In honor of the defeat of the French, this evening all the troops here paraded. The line formed on Broadway, near a mile long, and marched to the North River, where a *Feu-de-Joie* was made.

December 28*th. Tuesday.*—Last Thursday the fleet for England, said to be 130 sails, sailed from Sandy Hook. The expedition with Sir Henry Clinton and Lord Cornwallis has also sailed. The Hessian Gen. Knyphausen is in command here.

1780.

January 18*th. Tuesday.*—Yesterday we heard that the rebels were on Staten Island, where they plundered the people, burnt Decker's Ferry-house and several wood vessels which lay there. They remained one day on the island and returned with their spoils. The brig Hawk fired on them, and thereby prevented them from destroying another tavern and forage. It being the Queen's birthday, a salute was fired and at night the gentry had great festivities, which were carried too far in expense, in such times of distress

---

[1] *N. Y. Gazette*, October 25.

and calamity. It is said that the ball cost above 2000 Guineas, and they had over 300 dishes for Supper.[1]

January 27th. Thursday.—Some of our troops have been to Elizabethtown and Newark, & burnt it is said in the former place, the Barracks, a Meeting house; and in the latter a College or some public buildings used by the rebels. Seventy prisoners were brought in.[2]

February 4th. Friday.—This week sleighs have crossed over the ice from Staten Island to this city, which has hardly been known before.

March 21st. Monday.—Gen. Robertson who is appointed Governor of New York, arrived from England via Cork and Georgia. He reported Sir Henry Clinton with the army near Charleston.

April 17th. Monday.—We learned that about 200 Continentals were posted near Paramus to prevent desertions. 300 Hessians from King's Bridge and Buskirk, and about 100 Horse went thither, and yesterday before sunrise they surrounded the house in which they were. The post surrendered without opposition; in another, the Major answered to the summons that they would neither give nor take quarter, upon which the house was set on fire and many were killed as they ran out.

May 29th. Monday.—The news of the surrender of Charleston was brought by the Iris.

June 5th. Monday.—At night some fireworks were exhibited on Long Island, and here they had festivities. But previous thereto, the walk at Trinity Church had been increased in width, so that the posts had to be sunk into the graves. The orchestra from the Play House, seated against the Church, and another place for the musicians erected just opposite the Church, gave great offense and uneasiness to all serious and still more to all godly men, and caused

---

[1] Governor Tryon gave a dinner to Generals Knyphausen, Philips, Baron Reidesel, General Patison, commandant of the city, and others. The supper given by Mayor Hicks consisted of three hundred and eighty dishes, in addition to the ornamental appendages.

[2] *N. Y. Gazette,* January 31.

many reflections not only on the irreligious turn of the Commandant, but also on the Rector, who it is said had given his consent to it.   Profaneness and Wickedness prevaileth—Lord have mercy!

June 6th. Tuesday.—Today above 6000 Hessian and English troops went on an expedition, with the present commandant Gen. Knyphausen, and Gens. Robertson, Tryon, Mather &c.

June 7th. Wednesday.—Already by 4 o'clock in the morning smart firing was heard, which continued the greater part of the forenoon.   Some wounded were brought in, among them Gen. Stirling.

June 10th. Saturday.—Various reports were heard of our troops in the Jerseys.   It seems that some of the intelligence they had had here, had been given by a Spy, by which means our troops were led into an ambush; they fired also upon them from out of some houses, by which about 100 of our troops were killed and wounded.   In consequence several houses on the Connecticut farms were burnt.   However, our troops made room for themselves.

The Iris which sailed on Tuesday returned, having fallen in with a French frigate of 36 guns, which she obliged to sheer off, but an American frigate heaving in sight, and the Iris having lost some men and being a great deal damaged, she thought best to return to this port.   Their lieutenant was so badly wounded, he was brought on shore today.

June 17th. Saturday.—Admiral Arbuthnot arrived from Charleston yesterday, and was followed by Sir Henry Clinton, with part of the army.

June 23d. Friday.—From early in the morning till towards Noon, heavy firing was heard in the Jerseys, and afterwards the smoke from burning houses was seen for several hours. In the afternoon about 30 sails with troops, (of those returned from Charleston), came up from Staten Island, and proceeded up the North River.   This was an unexpected manœuvre.   The troops had been quartered on Staten Island about the Blazing Star,[1] from which it was conjectured that the intention was to march into the Jerseys.

[1] Clute's "Annals of Staten Island," p. 233.

June 24*th. Saturday.*—Some wounded were brought to the city, and we heard that our troops had left Elizabethtown and had returned to Staten Island. They embarked this forenoon, and in the afternoon passed the city and went up the North River. Washington some days ago had marched toward Paramus and the Cove. Gen. Knyphausen with a part of the troops marched forward and drove the rebels to Springfield, and it is said also to Chatham. They were mostly Militia, and stood and fought better than ever before. The bridge over the Kills to Staten Island was taken up. Various were the reflections! It is thought that Gen. Stirling's being wounded, caused the first delay and obstruction in the intended operations, that old Gen. R. had been a clog in the wheels, requesting a council of war, and objecting to penetrating into the Jerseys, or whatever was designed; that the return of Sir Henry perhaps had caused an alteration. Springfield was burnt.

June 26*th. Monday.*—A couple of regiments or parts of them, especially Hessians, came to the city, which relieved the citizens from duty. The guard over the prisoners in the North Church has been increased.

July 13*th. Thursday.*—The pleasing report was heard and confirmed that Admiral Graves with his fleet had reached the Hook, and consequently cometh pretty close after the French. This important news raised again the spirits of many which had been drooping, considering the unfortunate management of affairs here. It appears strongly that jealousy and a lack of harmony among the head men has been the cause why the late expedition into the Jerseys came again to nothing, and other such like things.

July 19*th. Wednesday.*—Admiral Arbuthnot having taken and manned what men-of-war are here, and got sailors enough as volunteers without pressing, sailed to-day from the Hook with a fair wind for Rhode Island, to meet the French fleet; at the same time Sir Henry Clinton and a part of the fleet prepared for embarking.

July 21*st. Friday.*—In the forenoon smart firing and cannonading was heard up the North River. A Refugee post (a block-house where the refugees cut wood) was attacked by near 2000 rebels, among them the 1st and 2d Battalions of Pennsylvania Brigades, under the Gens. Wayne and Irvine, with six pounders. They attempted to storm the abatis but were repulsed with a loss of 90 killed and wounded, and it is thought more. The Refugees were under command of Capt. Ward (refugee) and had 4 killed and 8 wounded. A part of them pursued the rebels, retook some cattle and captured a number of prisoners. They could not be succored from the opposite posts of troops, as there were no boats at hand. Their uncommon bravery has been acknowledged by the Commander-in-Chief in the public papers and they are to have uniform clothing and hats.[1]

July 26th. Wednesday.—Towards evening the Hessian General de Huyne was buried with military honors, attended by a vast concourse of people. He was in the expedition to Charleston, from whence he returned sick.[2]

August 1st.—Yesterday it was confirmed that Sir Henry Clinton and the troops had returned, which caused a painful disappointment to many, and various are the conjectures what the reason may be. It seems they were no higher up than Huntingdon, and that the Commander received intelligence on the return of the Galatea, that the French and rebels had fortified themselves so strongly on Rhode Island, that he could not attack them. Others think that it is on account of Washington's movements, who, by report, has been greatly reinforced. Perhaps the true reason is, that the embarkation was so tardy,—they might have started a week earlier, and why?—this is another question.

August 15th. Tuesday.—The heat in these days is almost unbearable.

August 24th. Thursday.—The Rope walk, above the Fresh

---

[1] For account of the attack on block-house at Bull's Ferry, and order of thanks, signed by John André, D.A.G., see *N. Y. Gazette,* July 24.

[2] Major-General de Huyne died on July 25 of consumption, in the sixtieth year of his age. He entered the army of Hesse-Cassel in 1738. The regiment of Donop and a company of Anspach grenadiers participated.

Water Pump, where there was stored Brimstone and other combustibles, burnt down tonight. The fire was violent, but did no damage to the surrounding property.[1]

September 14th. Thursday.—Admiral Rodney with 10 sails of the line, from the West Indies, arrived at the Hook yesterday. This is very unexpected news. We may now hope that something will be done. Many think that there has been bad conduct somewhere in respect to the first French fleet now in Rhode Island, and our fleet that followed.

September 22d. Friday.—It being the anniversary of His Majesty's, our dear Kings Coronation-Day, great rejoicings were made. Besides the usual firing at noon from the Battery, and 1 o'clock from the ships in the river, and at the Watering Place, in the afternoon all the City Militia, to a very great number, the volunteer companies, and a part of the regulars marched with flying colors out of town, and drew up in line from the East river to the North river, and in the evening a *Feu de Joie* was fired in respect to the day and in celebration of the brilliant victory obtained by Earl Cornwallis near Camden, in South Carolina. It was commenced by seven rockets, seven guns were then fired from the three batteries on Jones', Bunker's, and Lispenard's Hills.[2] Then followed the fire of the Line from right to left. The Commander-in-Chief, the noble Lords lately arrived with Admiral Rodney, the Governor, all the general and other officers, with a large concourse of people were present.

September 30th. Saturday.—This week the rebel Genl. Arnold came in.[3] The prevailing report is, that between him, having command of the Fort and that part of the county, and our side, a plan was formed to take Fort Defiance with the people in it, for which end Major André one of Sir Henry Clinton's aids went thither, but was taken on his re-

---

[1] Near Bunker Hill, and also noted on Montresor's map of 1775.

[2] See Montresor's map of 1775.

[3] "His Excellency the Commander-in-Chief has been pleased to appoint Benedict Arnold Esq. Colonel of a Regiment, with the rank of Brigadier General."—*N. Y. Gazette*, October 21.

turn. Upon hearing of this Gen. Arnold made off, got on board the Vulture, and thus to this city. At the same time a commotion was occasioned, and several persons in the city and on Long Island, were arrested and put in jail. The report was that Arnold had informed against them, as keeping a prejudicial correspondence with the rebels, but the truth is, that one Pool arrested as a spy some weeks ago and condemned, has impeached these persons. This he did to save his life.

October 7th. Saturday.—Gen. Robertson, a Colonel, Mr. Elliott and William Smith, as belonging to Sir Henry Clinton's collateral Council for making Peace, had by commission been to Gen. Washington's Head Quarters. They did not see him, nor were the two civilians allowed to go on shore. They were treated with contempt, and no Lieutenant-Governor or Chief Justice not of their own appointment would be recognized.

November 22d. Wednesday.—The Anspachers entered the North Church for Winter Quarters, and their Major, de Seitz, was billeted on us.

December 16th. Saturday.—The year is near ended and nothing has been done by the troops here. Many sensible and sincere well-wishers lament it with pain, whereas administration does so much for the American affairs. The troops thro' idleness fall into all manner of the worst of vices, contract illnesses, which take off many. Thus they dwindle away by that means, and by small excursions which answer no real purposes. After campaigns which have accomplished nothing, more troops are required. The general language even of the common soldiers is, that the war might and would have been ended long before now, if it was not for the great men, who only want to fill their purses; and indeed it is too apparent that this has been and is the ruling principle in all departments, only to seek their own private interest, and to make hay while the Sun shineth, and when they have got enough then to retreat or go home—let become of America what will!

December 23d. Saturday.—This week an expedition has

at length sailed, it is said for Virginia, Gen. Arnold in command.

1781.

January 6th. Saturday.—This week it was rumored that a considerable part of the Rebel army had revolted, owing to their time being out on New Year's day & not receiving their pay in *real* money. The report caused some excitement in the army here.

January 8th–13th.—Sir Henry Clinton with several thousand troops left Long for Staten Island, and the report is, that he is negotiating with the Revolters, who number now two thousand. However the reports vary often & the commander-in-chief keeps every thing very secret.

January 20th. Saturday.—The revolt of the Pennsylvania troops begins to dwindle away to nothing. Two messengers sent by Sir Henry Clinton were captured and hanged.

February 5th. Monday.—A frigate arrived from Virginia, which brought an account of Gen. Arnold's successful operations there. In this city robberies constantly take place; persons have been attacked on the streets, and a woman and a Scotch officer murdered—mostly by the soldiery. Poor discipline!

March 5th. Monday.—News was received that affairs in Virginia and Carolina are favorable. Lord Cornwallis had driven the rebels into Virginia, and Gen. Arnold was not surrounded as reported.

March 17th. Saturday.—This week news was received that the French fleet sailed from Rhode Island for Virginia, and that our fleet followed them. They were both seen near the bay, it was thought preparing for action.

March 26th. Monday.—Today an account was printed of an action between the English & French fleets off the Chesapeake. The latter were forced to return to Rhode Island. The English squadron entered the Bay which was fortunate, as Gen. Phillips with his troops from here arrived about the same time. The action was disgraceful on the British side; but three ships fought, which suffered considerably, and the French fleet slowly sailed away. The charge is laid to

Admiral Arbuthnot, who either forgot his business or was afraid to fight. However, it afterwards seemed that Admiral Graves was perhaps as blameable or more so.

April 5th. Thursday.—An account of a battle on the 15th or 16th of March, between Lord Cornwallis and the Rebel Gen. Greene, was published today. The Rebel army was defeated with a loss of about 1300 by their own account.[1]

April 23rd. Monday.—This week a fleet of victuallers arrived in Charleston; also a number of valuable prizes, among them the Confederacy, one of the best of the Rebel frigates.[2] On Saturday evening a *Feu de Joie* to celebrate Cornwallis' victory.

April 30th. Monday.—The Anspach, with two other regiments embarked today, and we are thus rid of the oppressive and disagreeable billet of the former. The conduct of the Major [Seitz] and his servants has been rude, and the rooms they occupied have been ruined.

May 19th. Saturday.—The news from Virginia this week informed us of the captures made in Virginia, and from Philadelphia, that great mobs there in formal procession buried the money current.

June 12th. Tuesday.—A fleet arrived from Virginia with Gen. Arnold and part of his command.

July 3rd. Tuesday.—Washington has advanced closer to our lines, and the French troops from Rhode Island have joined him. A party of rebels fell on a picket of several hundred Yagers & Hessians, a mile or more above King's Bridge, and killed & wounded a great many.

July 6th. Friday.—Admiral Arbuthnot has sailed for England in the Roebuck, and well it is, that he is gone, but it is a pity to take such a fine ship from this station. A fine brig, laden with rum and sugar, bound for this city was taken

[1] Guilford Court-House.

[2] The "Confederacy," 32, was launched near Norwich, Conn., in 1778, and Captain Seth Harding placed in command. In 1779, while conveying Hon. John Jay to Spain, she was dismasted near Bermuda. She was always an unlucky vessel, and at the time of her capture was laden with clothing and other supplies.

near the Hook and carried into Philadelphia, although our fleet lies about the Hook.

July 9th. Monday.—The heat continues intense and is the cause of much sickness.

July 13th. Friday.—Some days ago the French who joined the rebels under Washington and are at White Plains, sent a detachment to attack the fort at Lloyd's Neck, Long Island, which was repulsed.[1]

July 17th. Tuesday.—Yesterday an extraordinary Gazette was published of Lord Cornwallis' late operations in Virginia, and an action on the 6th inst. wherein the Marquis La Fayette was worsted and lost three cannon.

July 23rd. Monday.—We heard today that the Rebels were near King's Bridge, and that the French had driven the Refugees from Morrissania.   Fine attention !

July 28th. Saturday.—A rumor prevails that Admiral Digby has pursued the French fleet and recaptured six of their prizes.

September 1st. Saturday.—Troops under Gen. Arnold went up the Sound on an Expedition.   The principal object of this movement was to lure Washington from his operations against Cornwallis, and thus gain time to send reinforcements to Yorktown.   Admirals Graves and Hood sailed from the Hook.[2]   A French fleet from the West Indies has arrived in the Chesapeake.

September 11th. Tuesday.—Gen. Arnold has returned from his expedition.

September 13th. Thursday.—Today the 22d Regiment quartered in the North Church opposite to us went on board the transports.

September 15th. Saturday.—The troops which have been embarking this fortnight for Virginia, have fallen down the river.   This week Gen. Arnold with his troops returned from New London, which had been burned.

September 17th. Monday.—In an extraordinary Gazette an account of Gen. Arnold's expedition was published, giving his letter to Sir Henry Clinton; by which it appears that

[1] *N. Y. Gazette*, July 16.   [2] Ibid., September 3.

the burning of New London happened through intention (!);
that a great quantity of goods and stores were destroyed,
twelve vessels burned, and a large quantity of ordnance
and ammunition captured. That a powder-magazine in the
fort was ordered destroyed, but failed through mismanagement, it is said, of the commanding artillery officer. One
of the forts [Griswold] was found to be stronger than was
expected, through the information given by our friends,
and that in storming it we lost about fifty killed and 140
wounded. Among the former was Major Montgomery of
the 40th Regiment.

September 19th. Wednesday.—Admiral Graves with his fleet
arrived at the Hook from the Chesapeake, off which they
had had an engagement with the French fleet. Nothing
has been published, but it is reported that thirteen ships of
the line were engaged, and that the French were again in
the Chesapeake. The Terrible, 74, has been lost, and ten
of our ships will have to be refitted. How the French
fared no one knows, but it appears they had the best of the
engagement. In consequence of this affair the troops on
the transports were disembarked.

September 26th. Wednesday.—The July mail arrived with
the squadron of Admiral Digby which reached the Hook
yesterday; and this afternoon his Royal Highness, Prince
William Henry, the third son of our dear King came on
shore with the Admiral. He was received by Sir Henry
Clinton and the principal officers in the city, and escorted
by a guard of honor to his quarters, the guns at the batteries thundering forth a royal salute. He is an amiable
young Prince and gave satisfaction to all who saw him.[1]

September 27th. Thursday.—At noon Prince William Henry
with Sir Henry Clinton and his officers, walked from Headquarters to the Fort called Bunker's Hill, by the new road
and returned by the Bowery, passed the Fresh-water pump,

[1] Prince William Henry arrived on Monday, September 23. Lossing
states that the Prince (afterwards William IV.) and the Admiral occupied the city mansion of Gerardus Beekman, on the northwest corner of
Sloat Lane and Hanover Square, during their visit.

and then turned in at the head of Queen Street. The concourse of people, both old and young, was great.

October 13*th. Saturday.*—Last Sunday Prince William attended service at St. Paul's, in company with the Admirals and Sir Henry Clinton. It is said, this was the *first time* that the latter has been in a church. The fleet which was to return to the Chesapeake, is not ready yet, which has made people anxious. A heavy thunder gust today, and two men of war were damaged by collision in the North River.

October 17*th. Wednesday.*—In the forenoon the Grenadiers and Light Infantry, (in North Church) embarked.

October 18*th. Thursday.*—This afternoon the last of the fleet for Virginia drop'd down the Bay.

October 24*th. Wednesday.*—Yesterday and today, considerable firing was heard in the Jerseys, which was supposed to be rejoicing, and made our people very apprehensive of Cornwallis having been captured in Virginia. Our fears were confirmed later by a hand bill printed in Trenton. General consternation and lamentation prevailed.[1]

October 27*th. Saturday.*—The report of Lord Cornwallis' surrender was confirmed. This unfortunate event was caused through wilful neglect.

November 17*th. Saturday.*—This week the troops which had embarked for Virginia returned, likewise the fleet. Admiral Digby remains on this station, and consequently Prince William. The Hessian Grenadiers are quartered in North Church. A Proclamation of the Governor was issued to-day respecting fire-wood, which will afford much relief, for the distress and extortion has been great already. A brig was captured near the Hook by rebel whale-boats, though many men of war were near by.

November 24*th. Saturday.*—To-day Lord Cornwallis' letter to Sir Henry Clinton of October 20th, was published, doubtless at the demand of his Lordship. The letter reflects on

---

[1] On November 5 the *New York Gazette* reprinted the Postscript of the *Pennsylvania Journal* of October 24, containing the correspondence and articles of capitulation of Cornwallis and his army. The news of the surrender was received in Philadelphia on the morning of October 22.

the character of the Commander and Admiral-in-chief, and increases the indignation of the people. It shows that York and Gloucester were ordered to be taken, that relief had been promised in strong terms, and the date fixed, which induced his Lordship to remain and not endeavor to escape. The despatch giving his account of the surrender was withheld from the public, until just before his Lordship arrived here, which was on Tuesday last.[1]

December 11th. Tuesday.—Weather very cold; great distress for want of wood, the proclamations of no avail. According to the letters received in the last mail, the affair of Cornwallis is discussed everywhere, and that the campaign in these parts would end again in having done nothing. Warm work was expected in the House of Commons about the supplies, for the nation has grown tired of spending millions every year to no purpose; that it was apprehended the cause lay higher than in Admirals and Generals.

1782.

January 30th. Wednesday.—The cold last night and this morning was intense, and we could hardly keep warm near a large fire.

February 1st.—The rents of houses are again raised to extravagant figures.

April 20th. Saturday.—Many prizes have been brought into port recently, among them the Franklin, which had taken the Grenville Packet bound for Charleston, and carried her into Philadelphia.

May 5th. Sunday.—To-day Gen. Carleton arrived in the Ceres, frigate, with Mr. Watson Comr. Gen.; Capt Moss, Chief Engineer; Morgan, Secretary and Wroughton, Aid-de-Camp. A total change of the Ministry at home has taken place, and the opposition is in power. Rivington published a hand bill this evening.

May 12th. Sunday.—Last night news reached here of a severe engagement on April 12th, between the English

---

[1] For Cornwallis's letter to Clinton, see *N. Y. Gazette*, November 26.

under Admiral Rodney and the French fleet in the West Indies. Our vain chief printer had an account of it printed in hand-bills and cried about in the forenoon, while people were going to church—another catch-penny!

May 13*th. Monday.*—A rumor prevails that Washington has refused a pass to Sir Guy Carleton's secretary to go to Congress with the government's proposals for peace. About noon Sir Henry Clinton and Gen. Knyphausen went on board ship for England. A body of English and Hessian soldiers were drawn up in two lines from headquarters to the water side, near the lower barracks, through which the generals passed, escorted by a large number of officers. Numerous spectators were present. Gen. Knyphausen has the good wishes of all people, but Sir Henry leaves a poor character behind him.

May 18*th. Saturday.*—The new commander-in-chief makes many wholesome changes to the great saving of public expenses. It is said that a couple of hundred of Deputy Commissioners in different departments have been or will be dismissed, hundreds of carpenters and other workmen have been turned off; the office of Barrack and Quarter Master General will be vested in one person; no Commandant but the Governor, (it is said Gen. Patison); no officer will be allowed to have vessels, wagons, &c. to carry on any trade. We rejoice that the chain of enormous, iniquitous practices will be at last broken! They must have ended in misery to the nation, had they continued much longer. The inhabitants have also been relieved from working on the fortifications every fifth day.

May 20*th. Whit-Monday.*—A grand review of the troops was held this forenoon.

May 23*rd. Thursday.*—This morning the Refugee clergymen waited on the Commander-in-Chief. One of these gentlemen, chaplain of the 40th Regiment, was notified by the Major that he was to keep service for the regiment every Sunday at 8 o'clock—which has not been done for years past.

May 31*st. Friday.*—Prince William Henry, who it was

reported had sailed for England sometime since, returned to this city, having been on a cruise on the Warwick.

June 4th. Tuesday.—Our King's birthday. The Commander-in-Chief, with the General and field officers, both English and foreign, went from the parade to the Admiral's house and congratulated the Prince. The guns on the batteries and ships were fired as usual and the Admiral's ship gaily dressed with the colors of all nations. In the evening a *Feu de Joie* was fired, and some public buildings illuminated.

June 16th. Sunday.—Today the troops left the city to encamp, and the militia commenced to do duty.

August 4th. Sunday.—We learned that large numbers of gentlemen had called on the Commander-in-Chief and the Admiral relative to the news from England; that at the request of the inhabitants a copy of a letter from Sir Guy Carleton and Admiral Digby to Gen. Washington, written in consequence of orders from England, had been published. It cannot be described what an alarming effect this so unexpected news had upon the minds of the people; they were enraged against the Ministry. Some were for defending themselves to the last extremity and make their own conditions.

August 5th. Monday.—The militia refused to do duty any longer.

August 10th. Saturday.—About noon the Loyalists within the lines held a meeting in the Assembly Hall. The chairman Mr. Alexander offered an address and petition to the King, and another to the Commissioners, Sir Guy Carleton and Admiral Digby, for the approbation or dissent of those present. They were read and unanimously approved. Gov. Franklin was deputed to carry them to the King.

September 4th. Wednesday.—The July packet arrived. It is reported that the Marquis of Rockingham, late prime minister and a prominent member of the former opposition, and who had urged the independency of America, died on July 1st. Lord Shelburne has been appointed in his place, and he being opposed to independence, has caused

Mr. Fox, Secretary of State (an unhappy Tool), Mr. Burke, and others of the Rockingham party to resign. Parliament was prorogued for the 10th. However, all the news settles nothing with certainty about the fate of this country.

November 27th. Wednesday.—Today a fleet of Victuallers and Transports from England arrived. An account of Gov. Franklin's arrival and his gracious reception by the King; and the conference with him by the King and ministry on American affairs, was made public.

December 16th. Monday.—Greatest snow storm in thirty years.

1783.

January 4th. Saturday.—On the 2d. and the following days, a fleet arrived from Charleston, in which came Lieut. Gens. Leslie and de Bose, with a part of the troops, mostly Hessians, and some of the new corps. Some of the inhabitants came here, others with troops sailed for St. Augustine, Jamaica, Halifax and England.

January 18th. Saturday.—The Queen's Birthday—all was quiet—only Sir Guy Carleton gave a Ball.

January 27th. Monday.—It is said that all the prisoners on board the Prison Ships have been discharged and sent to their respective homes on parole. Among these was William Dunton of Philadelphia,[1] who was taken as mate in the Black Prince, merchantman, bound for Cadiz. While on board the Jersey Prison ship, he wrote to us to procure his liberty.

February 9th. Sunday.—Today a vessel arrived from Tortola, which brought the King's speech at the opening of Parliament, on Dec. 5th. It was re-printed by Rivington and published this evening.

February 11th. Tuesday.—A French vessel from Nantes, which left France 23d December, being brought in as a prize, renewed the alarm. She brought a note Mr. Townsend, Secretary of State, had sent to the Lord Mayor of

---

[1] He was a well-known sea-captain, and also a member of the Moravian congregation on Race Street, corner of Bread.

London d.d. Dec 3d., notifying him that an express from Paris had brought the preliminaries of a peace signed by the Ambassadors of France and of the United States of America. This note was printed in a hand bill this evening.

February 14*th. Friday.*—Several articles sold by auction have fallen surprisingly—Flour, Rum, Molasses, & Coffee (which once sold at 3s. per lb.), a sufficient proof the dearness in many things has been artificial. Some men will now meet with great losses, but deservedly, for their avarice and extortion.

March 1*st. Saturday.*—The soldiers have been lately employed in filling up and raising the grade in Trinity Church yard, it having grown too shallow for the graves, whence injurious effects were apprehended. Various reports of peace, and now a separate peace between England and America prevailed.

March 3*d. Monday.*—Yesterday a Ship with Spirits arrived from Jamaica, and by mismanagement or on purpose, she ran on the rocks near the Battery. She was unloaded to lighten her. Some of the rigging and 115 puncheons of Spirits were put on a sloop, which was carried off during the night. It is said to have been done by some of the Jersey people, but the general opinion is, that it was a designed matter done by people here.

March 17*th. Monday.*—Three mails have arrived. The whole city was now in agitation. The news afforded but little comfort to the Loyalists, and will if true, be a stain of the deepest dye upon the English nation, so long as history exists!

March 22*d. Saturday.*—The public affairs look gloomy. The Articles of Peace have been published more fully it is said, against the will of Congress. It is surprising what England gives up; it is shameful how the Loyalists are abandoned! To the hundreds who proposed to go to Nova Scotia, there is also a stoppage, for they hear that they can get no more than six months provisions, (those who went in the Fall received twelve months). Proceedings at home give but little encouragement to put any trust in such a government!

March 24th. Monday.—This week a report came from Philadelphia, which they had received there from the French Admiral Count D'Estaing, that the preliminaries of a peace had been signed on the 21st of January, which caused new alarm and grief, and more so as the articles as they appear are very bad, especially for the Loyalists, and for England too; giving away even a part of Canada, Penobscot &c.[1]

April 5th. Saturday.—A vessel arrived from London, which brought the account of peace being made. This increased the alarm.

April 8th. Tuesday.—At noon the King's Proclamation of the cessation of hostilities, was read at the City Hall, which had previously been done on board of the men-of-war and to the troops.[2]

May 3d. Saturday.—Many of those persons who left the city when the troubles began are returning.

June 4th. Wednesday.—The King's birthday was celebrated as usual.

August 25th. Monday.—Today the Light Horse went to Long Island, and other soldiers were sent elsewhere to protect the Loyal inhabitants against robberies and other abuses.

November 25th. Tuesday.—The soldiers in the Barracks just opposite our house marched off. Last night a strong watch was kept for fear of accidents or mischief. Today all the British left New York, and Gen. Washington with his troops marched in and took possession of the city.

November 29th. Saturday.—In the evening about 8 o'clock, we felt a slight shock of an earthquake; and about eleven, there was a more violent one, which shook all the city in a surprising manner. We felt it in bed—enough to arouse us from our first sleep.

[1] *N. Y. Gazette*, March 31.   [2] Ibid., April 7.